How to Teach
YOUR DOG
To Drive

Also by Mike Haskins

Drugs: A User's Guide

When In Rome: an alternative guide for travellers

We're All Doomed – a light-hearted guide to the
forthcoming multi-apocalypse

Numpty! A complete guide to loveable thickies

The Old Ones Are The Best

Wow I'm A Genieous!!! The Stupidest Things Ever Said
Online

Man Walks Into A Bar (Co-written with Stephen Arnott)

How to Teach YOUR DOG To Drive L

Mike Haskins

CONSTABLE · LONDON

CONSTABLE

First published in Great Britain in 2014 by Constable

Text copyright Mike Haskins, 2014
Images copyright © Richard Hocknell, Andy Jacobson,
Eleanor Haskins, Deb Hampson, John Hazler, Chris Naylor,
Adam and Gill Bullen, John Tierney and Shutterstock.

A CIP catalogue record for this book
is available from the British Library.

ISBN 978-1-47211-665-9 (paperback)
ISBN 978-1-47211-669-7 (ebook)

Typeset and designed in Great Britain by Design 23
Printed and bound in Great Britain by Clays Ltd, St Ives plc

Constable
is an imprint of
Constable & Robinson Ltd
100 Victoria Embankment
London EC4Y 0DY

An Hachette UK Company
www.hachette.co.uk

www.constablerobinson.com

Editor's note: Whatever you do, do not follow any of the advice or suggestions given in this book, which is completely stupid and contradictory from start to finish and highly dangerous to boot.

Foreword

by Dr. Cesar Milligan

(Founder of the Suffolk College of Teaching Your Dog How to Drive a Car)

The first dog I ever taught to drive a car was my aged Golden Retriever, George.

Poor old George had been a faithful companion to me for many years but he was getting a little long in the tooth at the age of twelve years old. (That's eighty-four in dog years). I had noticed that he didn't appear to enjoy his walks as he once had and that he was beginning to need my assistance so he could get up and hump the legs of my visitors.

One day my vet, Mr Raff, told me that George was having problems with his back legs. I was concerned. Could this be the end for my canine friend? I asked Mr Raff how George could continue to pursue his doggy interests.

'Simple,' the twinkly-eyed old vet told me. 'Get him a set of wheels.'

In retrospect, I realise that Mr Raff probably meant that I should get George some sort of specially made trolley on which he could park his backside and trundle himself along.

What the vet probably hadn't anticipated was that I would rush out and buy my dog a second-hand hatchback and devote the next few years of my life to trying to teach the smelly animal to drive. Nevertheless, that's what I did. And sure enough just four years (twenty-eight years in dog years) and about seven cars (forty-nine cars in dog cars) later I had succeeded.

Well, sort of.

To be honest, by that advanced age George was extremely doddery, and his poor old joints were getting stiff. And, of course, he had by now been involved in six or seven fairly serious traffic accidents. As a result he was quite slow moving. As indeed was my car. I was therefore increasingly unsure whether George was really driving the vehicle or if I had just managed to prop him up against the controls at the right angle for the car to start moving forwards.

Sometimes the car moved. Sometimes it stayed still. I have to admit there was little in the way of mixing and matching as regards old George's use of

the brake and accelerator pedals. It was always one or the other with him. Never a mixture of the twain. He either stayed completely stationary or began moving forward at an ever-increasing speed.

Sadly, George's days were numbered. However I had developed a real passion for teaching dogs to drive, and that's why I established the Suffolk College of Teaching Your Dog How to Drive a Car.

For years now I have been teaching dogs to drive and I believe that I can say with justification that no one has had more success than myself at getting dogs through the driving examination – both practical and written elements. Admittedly, I haven't had much success at all. But I don't think anyone else has had more success. And at least I've had a go!

I have put more dogs in the driving seat of cars than anyone else alive. And if you don't believe me I can show you my receipts from car repair shops, scrap dealers, vets and the RSPCA (not to mention the car valet services for removing stains from the driver's seat).

And the reason I do it is because dogs love driving

cars. They sit with their little paws propped up on the steering wheel while they speed down the high street, along a country lane or just straight through someone's garden. And passers-by love to see dogs driving. Particularly if they are watching from a safe vantage point.

Passengers are often less keen.

And there are some people who find the whole practice of training a dog to drive a large motorised vehicle highly controversial in the first place;

They claim it is dangerous.[1]

They suggest it should be illegal.[2]

They think dogs are simply not capable of driving cars.[3]

So, just who are these killjoys?[4]

What harm can a St Bernard or a German Shepherd or even a little Chihuahua really do when driving at speed through a densely populated area?[5]

When I tell friends that I have successfully taught my Golden Retriever George to drive the family

---

1 *Editor's note: That's because it is dangerous.*

2 *Editor's note: It is illegal.*

3 *Editor's note: Once again it is hard to fault their logic.*

4 *Editor's note: The overwhelming majority of sane, normal people.*

5 *Editor's note: A considerable amount. A dog placed in control of a moving car can do an extraordinary amount of damage even on a relatively short journey.*

motor they immediately exclaim, 'My goodness! How extraordinary!' Then after a moment's thought they will ask, 'How exactly do you define "successfully" in this case?' And then may add in a shrill voice, 'Actually, could you just stop the car here? Don't worry about giving me a lift to the station. Now I come to think of it, I quite fancy a walk instead.' A period of frantic fumbling at the car door handle then follows before they tumble out of the moving vehicle and roll into a ditch.

But I have no sympathy for these doubters. I have devoted the past fifty-six dog years of my life (that's eight years in human years) to teaching dogs to drive. It is my heartfelt belief that dogs are perfectly capable of controlling a moving vehicle. I don't care what arguments are put forward by the nay-sayers and the gloom-mongers and their so called 'overwhelming scientific evidence to the contrary'.

So come on, dog lovers! Strap Fido into the front seat of your car and let's hit the road, doggy-o![6] Then just watch the unalloyed joy spread over his hairy

---

6 *Or for owners of female dogs: 'Strap Fifi into the front seat of your car and let's hit the road, bitchy-o!']*

little face. Particularly as this will be sticking out of the side window as he goes speeding off. And suddenly the number of pensioners who keep bouncing off the bonnet will seem worth it.

Yes! Lets get these dogs driving!

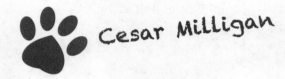

What Characteristics of Dogs Make Them Ideal Drivers?

Dogs are loyal

Dogs are loyal companions. They won't abandon you midway through a journey, as a cat might if you tried to get them to drive you anywhere. But then what sort of idiot would teach a cat to drive?

Dogs enjoy learning to perform tasks

With patience you can teach your dog to fetch a ball, to shake hands or to roll over. It will only take that little bit of extra patience to teach him how to drive a car.

Dogs like to work

Many dogs were bred as working animals, who traditionally gained satisfaction and confidence from performing tasks for their owners. Giving your dog the job of driving you around in a car is only slightly different from teaching a dog to round up sheep or sniff out heroin in airport luggage.

Dogs like to please their owners

And what better way can your dog please you than by acting as your designated driver?

Dogs are tenacious

Dogs are tenacious and determined. They will keep driving no matter what, and have greater stamina than even an Eastern European taxi driver. They are very unlikely to stop and ask for directions. Being driven by a dog is therefore very similar to being driven by a man except for the fact that dogs have a better sense of direction.

Dogs like moving objects

Dogs love anything that moves. And where are you going to find more moving objects than on a busy road?

Dogs are tactile

Dogs love chewing and playing with various toys and other objects. This means they will love learning to use the controls of your car. However, they will tend to operate them with their mouths rather than their paws.

Dogs are covered in fur

Your dog's paws are furry, which means they will never need driving gloves in the winter.

Getting Started

1. Sit your dog in the driver's seat of the car. This is clearly the best place for him to be if you want him to do the driving. Teaching a dog to drive is difficult enough but trying to control a moving vehicle while sitting in any seat other than the driver's seat is particularly challenging – as I am sure we have all found out to our cost.

2. When your dog hops up into the driver's seat, wait while he turns round three times before finally sitting down.

3. After turning round three times in a little circle, make sure your dog has ended up facing in the right direction. (He should be sitting in the seat

looking forwards out of the front windscreen – I know this kind of stuff is obvious to us but it may be less obvious to your dog).

4. If your dog is quite small you may have to put a cushion under him. It's no good if he is facing in the right direction but he is too low down to see out of the windscreen. If you have a ridiculously small dog you may need to balance him on top of six or seven cushions. Please note that this could lead to your dog tumbling to the floor in an avalanche of soft furnishings the first time the car turns a corner.

5. Strap your dog in using the seatbelt – for humans the seatbelt acts as a safety device, providing a restraint in the event of sudden impact. For your dog it will be even more useful: it will hold him firmly in place in the driver's seat; it will prevent him from turning round again during the journey and ending up facing the wrong way; and it will keep him from jumping out of the window or leaping into the back seat when he sees something he doesn't like coming towards him in the front windscreen.

6. Prop your dog's front paws up on the steering wheel – your dog will initially find it less easy to grip the steering wheel than you do because of his lack of opposable thumbs. Resist the temptation to use duct tape as this may hinder your dog's ability to change gear.

7. Switch on the ignition.

8. Make sure there is no one around – on the road, in the vicinity or in sight – and that there are no sharp bends, walls or steep drops immediately ahead.

9. Instruct your dog to depress the clutch, put the car into gear and gently apply pressure to the accelerator.[1] Have an extra large doggy treat ready to stuff in his mouth if he is in any way successful. This should (eventually) make the complicated sequence of actions that he needs to perform stick in his little mind.

10. If your dog has still not managed the above manoeuvre after a few hours, and your car has been running in neutral for so long you have had to

---

1 *Editor's note: Yeah, good luck getting Fido to do this one!*

re-fill the tank more than three times, you may have to consider squeezing down under the driver's seat so you can work the pedals for your dog.

11. Alternatively you can just prop the accelerator down with a brick and he should start moving off – increasingly quickly!

12. The car should now be moving forwards.

13. That's it. Congratulations!
You have successfully got your dog driving.

14. So, is that it? Is the rest of the book going to be nothing but blank pages with the word 'Notes' printed at the top?

15. Well, to be honest, it is arguable whether what your dog is doing really constitutes driving. Some people might argue that all you have done is strap a helpless animal inside a vehicle and set it moving in a way that could cause injury to the dog, passers-by and surrounding property. And, unfortunately, this is almost certainly how the police, the courts and animal protection services will view the situation.

16. This means that we are going to need a few more lessons before we can declare your dog entirely ready to set out on the open road . . .

Reasons for Wanting to Teach Your Dog How to Drive – No. 1

Your dog is exceptionally intelligent

Dogs are highly intelligent creatures. Mental stimulation keeps them happy, healthy and well-balanced. And what more mental stimulation can you  offer your dog than to get him to drive through town in the middle of the rush hour?

Controlling a car in the middle of busy traffic will give your dog's brain a thorough workout.[2]

---

2 *Editor's note: And it will probably do the same for all the other drivers who happen to be on the road at the same time.*

What to Do if Your Dog Doesn't Realise He Is the Driver

Imagine this. An owner wants to get his dog driving. He sits the dog in the driver's seat of his car. He switches on the ignition, releases the handbrake and helps his canine companion put the car into gear. The loving owner may even give the car a little push or position it at the top of an incline to get it moving. The vehicle moves off, his dog looks happily out of the window as the car begins speeding up. A few seconds later it slams into a wall and poor old Rover has his face stuck in a recently inflated airbag.

Let's take a closer look at what went wrong in this scenario. There are many possible explanations, but perhaps one of the most significant is as follows.

The dog driver had no understanding whatsoever that he was meant to be in control of the car during its short journey!

Even after the journey came to its abrupt conclusion, the dog may still not have realised that he could have done anything to avert the final impact. And who can blame the poor mutt? Dogs are used to being driven around in a car. No one has ever told them that the person sitting in the front seat holding the steering wheel is the one responsible for controlling the car.

However, if the driver sitting in the driving seat of a moving car doesn't realise he or she is supposed to be driving and is thus in control of the speed, direction and braking of the vehicle, this is likely to be a problem.

There are several reasons why this problem may arise for a human driver. Let's examine them first.

Reasons Why Human Drivers May Fail to Realise They Are Supposed to Be in Control of the Vehicle They Are Currently Driving

1. They are extraordinarily drunk.

2. They have gone a bit funny in their old age.

3. They have nodded off at the wheel.

4. They are extremely unobservant.

5. They are so stupid and/or absent-minded that they have completely forgotten they were supposed to be driving.

They have spent their entire life in a tribe living in a remote part of the Brazilian rainforest and have therefore never seen a car before and yet have just been placed in the seat of a moving vehicle. Unfortunately, this problem occurs more frequently with dog drivers. This is odd because there are statistically much fewer reasons for the situation to arise with a dog driver.

Reasons Why a Dog Driver May Fail to Realise He Is Supposed to Be in Control of the Vehicle He Is Currently Driving

1. He is a dog.

So what can be done to solve this difficulty?

Ways to Teach Your Dog that He Is in Control of Your Car

1. Sit him in the driving seat, set him off driving and tell him he is a 'bad boy' every time the car crashes. Eventually, he should begin to realise there is something he should be doing, and start driving the car. Either that or he will become increasingly reluctant to get in the car in the first place, in which case you may have to move on to other methods.

2. Drive with him sitting on your knee with his paws propped up on the steering wheel until he gets the hang of things.[3] Of course, if you have a large dog, you won't easily be able to see out of the windscreen. Without due care and attention this may lead to you using your dog as a hairy dog-shaped airbag.

3. Stick something on the bonnet of the car that your dog will be interested in moving towards. You could try a large tasty bone, your dog's favourite squeaky toy or just superglue a cat to the front of

---

3 Editor's note: DO NOT DO THIS! IT WOULD BE AN INCREDIBLY DANGEROUS THING TO DO.

your car.[4] You'll be surprised how quickly your dog picks up the ability to drive then.

4. *Build up your dog's experience of driving through a series of smaller vehicles. Start by teaching your dog to hop onto a skateboard.*

Next get him used to a small trolley and then eventually work your way up until he is ready to hop into a Ford Fiesta and guide it down the road. Your dog will thus become gradually accustomed to the idea of steering and controlling the vehicle. Be warned, however, that when he wants to stop, he may be tempted to jump out of the car door rather than applying the brake properly.

4 *Editor's note: I'm starting to wonder why I'm bothering, but this would clearly be cruel and illegal and is terrible advice all round.*

Reasons for Wanting to Teach Your Dog How to Drive – No. 2

Your eyesight is failing

People who are partially sighted are given specially trained guide dogs to assist them as they walk down the street. This practice has been going on for years and is universally regarded as a wonderful thing. But guide dogs were invented years ago when everyone had to walk everywhere.

These days going on foot is simply not practical for most journeys. The shops are too far away. Town planning is carried out on the assumption that the majority of journeys will be taken by car. And many pedestrians find it difficult to cross the road even if they can see perfectly. So surely it is perfectly legitimate to update the idea of the guide dog to a driving dog who will drive the partially sighted around wherever they want to go. And if we can all agree on that[5] then why restrict it just to the partially sighted?

Why not broaden the range of people eligible for dog drivers to those who are slightly short-sighted or

---

5 *Editor's note: No, we cannot all agree on this asinine suggestion.*

who have a bit of difficulty reading the small print, or just those of us who can't remember where we left our glasses?

Or, if the decision is made to restrict this option to the genuinely partially sighted you could keep a white stick in the car anyway. To make the point clearly, while being driven along by your dog reach out of the passenger window and use your stick to tap along the side of the pavement.[6] Then surely no one will dare challenge your right to the simple pleasure of allowing your dog to drive!

---

6 *Editor's note: Ignoring the fact that this is in very poor taste, it may also cause you to break your arm.*

How to Acquaint Your Dog with the Controls in Your Car

When your dog starts driving he will probably have no interest in any of your car's controls. He will not care about the difference between the vehicle's gear stick, hand brake, pedals, steering wheel, indicators, headlight switch, windscreen-washer button, etc.

If the driver of a vehicle is oblivious to the existence and purpose of a car's controls this can lead to problems during the course of a journey. You must therefore make some attempt to fix your dog's attention on the controls.

You can start by detaching, unscrewing or snapping each of the controls in turn from your car. Then take them to the park with your dog. Once in the park you can get your dog interested in the car's controls through play. You can use the gearstick, for example, in a tug of war, or use your steering wheel as a giant Frisbee and throw it across an open area for your dog to run after and retrieve.

This may get your dog interested in your car's controls but it may also mean that when reattached, your steering wheel and gear stick are bent,

half-eaten and peppered with doggy tooth marks.

Don't worry about this as you won't have much choice in the end. Your dog will almost certainly prefer to use his mouth to work the car's controls. There are two reasons for this. Firstly, because he is a dog. And, secondly, since he is a dog he lacks opposable thumbs and thus has to grip the controls with his mouth rather than his paws.

What to Do If Your Dog Lacks Opposable Thumbs

No, don't bother checking. Dogs just don't have them.

The lack of opposable thumbs may pose problems when teaching your dog to use the controls in your car. You can try using some form of artificial thumb made from a vegetable or simply from discarded human thumbs. These can be attached to your dog's paws.

In my experience, however, artificial thumbs do not tend to be particularly effective and may even drop off during the course of a drive. And if one or more of your thumbs drops off while you are driving, it can be dangerous.

It is probably better to get used to the idea that dogs use their mouths for many of the things for which we might prefer to use our hands. So when your dog is driving he will use his mouth to perform tasks such as changing gear, switching on the indicators, changing the channel on the radio and scratching his bottom.

On the downside this means that for much of the time while he is driving your dog will not be looking at the road ahead but will instead be nosing around the dashboard and using his mouth to nudge the controls into the correct position.

On the plus side this helps significantly when you are teaching your dog to drive, as you can use tasty treats to get his interest, as we shall see next.

Encouraging Your Dog to Drive Using Tasty Treats

The best way to continue teaching your dog about the controls is often to smear each of them with tasty treats and titbits. Cheese, salami and bits of chicken can be wiped over the switches, knobs and other car controls.

Do not make the mistake of smearing all the controls in the car with treats on your dog's first drive. If you do so, your dog may go into a frenzy as soon as he climbs into the vehicle. He will begin attacking, biting and licking the controls just as he is pulling out into traffic. And this could result in a hazard.

It may therefore be better to teach your dog to drive by smearing each of the controls with food one by one. In order to do this in a controlled manner, you should teach your dog to use one of the controls at a time. For several journeys concentrate exclusively on the indicators and smear these with pâté every time you go out.

Then exclusively concentrate on smearing the clutch with a sausage for the next few journeys.

And then exclusively concentrate on smearing the back windscreen de-mister switch for the next few journeys.

And so on.

Obviously this innovative teaching technique is not without problems. It may mean that you will have to make several car journeys during the course of which your dog driver will attempt to control the vehicle using nothing other than the back windscreen de-mister button. Nevertheless, with firm and patient instruction your dog will quickly get the idea of how to use each of the controls in turn.

Then it will be a simple matter of getting him to bring all this knowledge together and use all of the many controls at the appropriate moment while driving at speed through a busy environment.

Reasons for Wanting to Teach Your Dog How to Drive – No. 3

You keep getting lost in the new ring road system

Dogs are always able to find their way home. So if you get lost anywhere, pop your pooch in the driving seat and he will quickly guide you homewards.

Bear in mind that he may not drive the right way down the one-way system on the way but he will eventually get you there.

Dogs navigate using their highly acute sense of smell. This will be aided by your dog's own personal scent marks that he will have left along the route during the outward journey.

As we all know, dogs wee every few steps when they are out on a walk. Dogs in cars have to adopt a slightly different strategy. They will again wee at regular stages during the course of a drive. They clearly prefer this to using a sat nav. But when weeing from a car, dogs of course have to cock their legs up and aim out of the side window. So always remember to wind Rover's window down to be ready for this.

Weeing out of the car window will of course spray

other cars, cyclists and pedestrians who happen to be passing by at the time. On the plus side, however, it will mean that your dog's wee is spread over a much larger area than if you were going by foot. And this will make it even easier for your dog to find the way back home.

So if you have a dog, why bother buying that expensive new sat nav?

Your Dog's First Proper Drive Using All the Controls

Once you have taught your dog the use of each of the controls in the car, sit next to him in the passenger seat and get him to set off on a drive.

Have your range of treats ready but hold them securely, or keep them in a sealed Tupperware container, so your dog doesn't immediately jump on top of you and start trying to prise them from your grasp as you are travelling along a busy road at 70 mph (and, don't forget, that is 490 in dog mph).

Then whenever it becomes necessary to use one of the controls, produce one of your treats, smear it over the relevant controls and tell your dog 'Good boy!' Point to the smeared control while doing this. Your dog should then perform the necessary action to change gear, switch on the indicators, perform an emergency stop, or whatever operation is currently necessary.

If you are travelling through a busy driving environment such as a town centre or motorway interchange it may be necessary to use a number of controls in a short space of time. In these circumstances you will need to be very handy when smearing the car controls with tasty treats. Your hands will be a blur as they flash over the dashboard and down to the pedals wiping a bit of cheese on the indicators, a piece of salami on the brake pedal and some minced morsels on the gear stick.

Don't forget, however, that after a period of smearing the controls with tasty treats, your car may become malodorous. If the odour becomes too strong it may cause your dog to froth saliva from his mouth while he drives.

Also, watch out for packs of hungry dogs chasing after your car as you drive past them.

Finally, don't forget that smearing sausages, cheese and other items over your car controls may make them slippy. After an intensive driving session your car may be dripping with oils and dog saliva and if you immediately hop into the driving seat yourself the controls may slip in your hands, thereby causing a serious accident.

It is important to avoid this, because if your dog sees you being involved in a head-on collision, it may inappropriately influence his perception of the correct way to drive.

Reasons for Wanting to Teach Your Dog How to Drive – No. 4

Your dog is less annoyed by other drivers than you are

Dogs are simple creatures at heart. They always see the best in others, whereas we humans may suffer stress and anxiety, leading us to lose patience and see ill in our fellow man.

This may particularly manifest itself on the road. We can become increasingly upset or even irate if other drivers push in front of us, overtake us on the inside lane or fail to give us a little wave of thanks when we have waited to let them pass through a narrow gap. Such things will, however, hardly trouble a friendly dog whose tail will still be wagging behind him on the driver's seat even if a foul-mouthed youth pulls out in front of him while flicking Vs out of the window.

Of course, there are exceptions. If your dog is overtaken by a postman in a Royal Mail van, do prepare yourself for a bit of canine road rage.

Ideal and Less Ideal Places for Your Dog to Begin His Driving Tuition

 ## Ideal Place

A very wide, quiet road

Less Ideal Place

A very narrow, busy one-way street on which you are currently facing in the wrong direction

 A large open car park area that is currently closed to other vehicles

The top level of a tall multi-storey car park with inadequate barriers around its edges

 A road with no other road users in sight

The road immediately outside your local police station

 A straight road that travels for miles through flat open landscape

A bendy, poorly lit cul-de-sac with large brick walls on each side and another large brick wall across the road just round the final bend

 An area with few distractions for your dog

The road past your local butcher's, the sausage factory and cat sanctuary

 An island with no other people or vehicles on it

An island with a precipitous cliff face all the way round it

Staying Calm While Your Dog Is at the Wheel

It is advisable to stay calm whenever your dog is driving and you are travelling with him as a passenger. Panicking, screaming, shouting and crying may be natural responses during the early stages of teaching your dog to drive, but this kind of behaviour may distract your dog while he is attempting to master the salami-smeared controls of your car.

Imagine yourself in your dog's place for a moment: Someone panicking, screaming and shouting in the passenger seat would probably distract you too, no matter how experienced a driver you are.

Remember – if you show signs of tension, your dog will become tense in turn. He may then become excitable and difficult to bring back under control. You do not want this situation to occur under any circumstances. You particularly do not want it to occur when you are heading towards a busy junction at speed with your dog in the driver's seat.

In such circumstances it will seem entirely natural to shout, swear and scream at the top of your voice. But this is the last thing you should do. Instead you need to somehow remain completely impassive.

As you hurtle towards the moving traffic simply keep repeating the command that you want your dog to perform. Express the command simply in as few words as possible so your dog will understand.

Keep repeating slowly and calmly: 'Brake . . . Brake . . . Brake . . . Good boy . . . Brake . . . Brake . . .'.

Do not expect your dog to brake successfully on the first attempt. Each time he does manage to brake in time make a big fuss of him and feed him a choccy drop.

If you remain calm and praise your dog each time he manages to avoid an accident, it shouldn't take too many attempts before he begins to get the hang of things.[7]

---

7 *Editor's note: Is there some way we can get out of publishing this book? Can someone get in touch with the legal department to look at the contract again?*

Reasons for Wanting to Teach Your Dog How to Drive – No. 5

Your arms and legs are slightly too short to reach the controls of the car

Anyone who faces such a challenge in their life as short arms or legs should surely not be denied the services of a dog chauffeur. How else could these people drive in safety and comfort? (OK, maybe they could just adjust their seat so it's a bit nearer the controls. But isn't it easier all round to simply provide them with a canine chauffeur?)

Anyone who wants to prevent people with shorter than average arms being driven around by their dogs is surely guilty of the most appalling prejudice. In fact they are probably in breach of the Human Rights Act.[8]

---

8 Editor's note: This is extremely unlikely to be the case. Please, never take advice from barrack room lawyers like this, they rarely know what they are talking about.

What to Do If Your Dog Insists On Driving with His Head Sticking Out of the Side Window

Dogs like to stick their heads out of the window when they are travelling in a car. This allows their ears and jowls to flap and blow around in the breeze. It is therefore likely that if your dog takes up driving he will adopt a similar position and drive with his paws on the steering wheel while his head sticks out of the side window.

On the plus side this will enhance your dog's enjoyment of the drive, it will give him a clearer view of the road ahead and it will save you having to teach him how to use the windscreen wipers or screen-wash squirter button.

On the downside it is quite a dangerous position in which to drive. Try driving with your own head sticking out of the window and observe what happens.[9]

Firstly, you will quickly develop a severe neck ache.

---

9 Editor's note: Do I really need to say? Don't do this! It is an utterly stupid thing to do!

You will also notice rain and small stones from the road surface constantly being blown up into your face.

You will also be regularly clubbed and bumped about the head by cyclists and pedestrians passing too close to the side of your vehicle.

And, of course, something worse may happen if another driver whizzes past you at too great a speed. Your decapitated head may then be left with a surprised expression all over its face as it stares at the driver of a sports car who had thought the road was a little bit wider than it actually was.

Driving with your head sticking out of the side window will also make turning left a hazardous and potentially lethal manoeuvre.

And if all that isn't bad enough, if anyone accidentally presses the button to close the window your head will be lifted up to the top of the door while you are slowly throttled. And that may distract you from your driving.

These dangers exist even for advanced drivers who attempt to drive with their heads stuck out of the side window. For a dog driver, additional dangers exist.

For instance, if your dog sees a cat walking down the side of the road, he may hop out of the open side window to chase it on foot. This will leave you travelling at high speed with no one in the driving seat at all.

You should therefore discourage your dog from driving with his head sticking out of the side window. Wind the windows up,[10] strap him in securely and do not teach him how to open the window himself.

If your dog is upset by this then pile a few cushions beneath him and let him drive with his head sticking out of the open sunroof. That way he should have a better view on both sides of the car, there will be less danger of him jumping out or being decapitated by another car, and he will still be able to enjoy the wind whistling through his blubbery jowls.

Unfortunately, he may then be sitting too high up to see or reach the steering wheel and other controls. But you can't have everything.

---

10 Editor's note: Hang on! Doesn't this contradict the earlier utterly idiotic advice about leaving the window open so your dog can urinate out of it?

What to Do If Your Dog Insists on Driving with His Head Sticking Out of the Side Window

Reasons for Wanting to Teach Your Dog How to Drive – No. 6

You are currently banned from driving

You have been banned from driving but you still need to get to the shops or be dropped off at work. If no human family members are willing and able to take you, surely it is acceptable to get your dog to drive you instead.

Old Rover hasn't ever been banned from driving has he? He doesn't have any penalty points on his licence. Well, he probably doesn't even have a proper licence. Which brings us on to the next problem . . .

How to Legally[11] Get Your Dog Through the Driving Test

It can be a challenge trying to get a driving licence for your dog.[12]

But there are a couple of options available.[13] Firstly, you can try and get your dog successfully through the driving test. This may present a challenge for several reasons.

1. It is very difficult to teach anyone, let alone a dog, how to drive a car.[14]

2. It is not currently legal for your dog to apply even for a provisional licence. Those of us devoted to teaching dogs to drive naturally regard this as a pernicious prejudice perpetuated in law.

3. Even if you manage to trick the DVLA into giving your dog a provisional licence he may still run into

---

11 Editor's note: There are no circumstances under which this will be legal.
12 Editor's note: It is not a challenge. It is illegal. Even applying to get your dog a licence is illegal. You will be arrested for wasting people's time. Do not even think about doing this.
13 Editor's note: There are no options available.
14 Editor's note: It is not difficult; it is impossible to teach a dog to safely drive a car! Please can we just take this point as read for the remainder of the book?

problems when he arrives at your local driving test centre to take his test. It is possible that some driving examiners will abandon the test immediately when they see that they are going to be driven around for the next half hour by a dog.

4. Even if you think you can teach your dog to drive, and you succeed in getting him a provisional licence, and you also somehow get him through the practical driving test, a significant challenge still remains. These days, as well as having to do a practical driving test, driving candidates have to sit a written test. So even if you successfully get your dog through all the other elements involved in the examination, you will also have to teach him to read.

5. Teaching a dog to understand language and read is something of a challenge in itself. But do not despair. I am currently working on a follow-up to this volume, entitled *How to Teach Your Dog to Read*, provisionally scheduled for publication in 2015.[15]

------

15 *Editor's note: Over my dead body. Can someone get an injunction taken out to prevent this author from coming anywhere near my office again?*

Getting Your Dog a Driving Licence Slightly Less Legally

This is a marginally easier option than trying to get your dog through the normal driving test. When you apply for a driving licence it is necessary to fill in a form. If it is immediately clear to the DVLA from the name given on the form that the applicant is a dog they may decide not to issue a licence.

So what can you do to avoid this problem?

1. Avoid getting your dog to fill in the form himself. If there is a muddy paw print next to questions such as 'What is your name?' this will be an instant giveaway to the DVLA that the driving applicant is a dog and your canine friend will probably not be issued with a licence.

2. Avoid filling in your dog's actual name on the form. If a member of the DVLA staff opens your application and sees a name at the top of the form such as Rover, Spot, Jack Russell, Fred Bassett, Hairy MacLary, Rex Barker or Mr Wuff Wuff McDoggy-Biscuits, they may again be quick to deduce that the applicant is a dog.

3. Instead it may be better to fill in the form slightly less truthfully. You could begin, for example, by using a cunning pseudonym.

Cunning Pseudonyms that You Might Want to Use On Your Dog's Driving Licence Application:

Jermaine Shepherd

Alice Atian

Del Mation

Steph Ordshire-Terrier

Sall Uki

Rod Esian-Ridgeback

Lars R. Apso

Saint Bernard

King Charles Spaniel

Dick Shund

Old Ian Gliss-Sheep-Dogg

Y. Maraner

Bill Doug

Gordon Setter

Otto Hound

Goldie N. Retriever

Pat R. Dale-Terrier

Rod Weiller

Stan Dard-Poodle

Shit Sue

Jack Russell

Bernie Smountain-Dogg

Irish Wilf Hound

B. Gull

Pat Bull-Terrier.

Please note it is possible that certain eagle-eyed officials at the DVLA may spot what is going on if you use these sorts of names and as a result they may start asking some very awkward questions about Mr Pat Bull-Terrier.

4. So it may be better to fill in the form using a plain and ordinary-sounding name. It is important to remember that using a false name on the application form may lead to problems down the line. If the driving examiner at the practical test keeps referring to your dog as Mrs O'Shaughnessy, Doctor Michael Travers or Sir Norbert Carnegie III, rather than by his proper name, this may cause your dog to become confused. For example, when the examiner tells your dog, 'When I tap the dashboard, Mrs O'Shaughnessy, I want you to imagine a child has run out in front of the car and for you to bring the car to an emergency halt,' your dog may not realise the instruction was intended for him.[16]

---

16 Editor's note: Have we heard back from the legal department about getting an injunction on this author yet? Perhaps we should also contact social services?

5. You may also have to disguise your dog for the picture on his photo card. These days, driving licences include a small photo of the licence-holder. If you are taking out a licence for your dog you will need to send a picture of him to the DVLA with his application form. If the DVLA receive your application with a photo of a dog's face, this again may give the game away.

Reasons for Wanting to Teach Your Dog How to Drive – No. 7

You cannot afford a proper chauffeur

Let's say that you have delusions of grandeur but you are on a budget. What other option is there but to pop a chauffeur's cap on your dog and let him drive you to that swanky party or business meeting?

It is probably best to have your car fitted with tinted windows though. It will not make the ideal impression if your rich friends and business associates see you being driven around by a hairy, malodorous old dog.

Reasons for Wanting to Teach Your Dog How to Drive – No. 8

You are an appalling alcoholic

This may seem a slightly dodgier argument for teaching your dog to drive than (for example) being partially sighted.

On the other hand, you will have heard people describe you as being 'blind drunk'. So clearly the two conditions aren't so different after all.

Many people also like to drink until they are in a state that they describe as 'paralytic'. Who could possibly argue against someone who is paralytic being denied assistance with their mobility even if this assistance is only provided in the form of a dog chauffeur?[17]

Also we all know that we must not drive if we have been drinking. So letting your dog drive you home after a few pints in the pub will surely be safer than trying to do it yourself.

Unless of course your dog has been drinking as well.

---

17 Editor's note: You know what, if we really have to put up with this, I want no further part in it. I didn't come into publishing to make trash like this. I thought I'd be making proper books for decent people. Nice leather-bound books by Martin Amis and Julian Barnes. Books I could talk to people about at fancy dinner parties. As it is, I'm embarrassed to admit what I do these days. I tell people I'm a street sweeper just so I can avoid talking about 'what I do for a living', and it's all the fault of idiot authors like this one.

What to Do If Your Dog Keeps Steaming the Windscreen Up

Having a dog sitting at the front of the car can result in an ongoing battle between the dog's breath and the car's windscreen de-mister. But, as we have already established, if you open up the side window to let a bit of fresh air in, your dog's head will be straight out of it.

The only solution is to turn the de-mister up to maximum, or perhaps rig up a dehumidifier on the dashboard to soak up your dog's slobbery breath.[18]

---

18 Editor's note: OK, after some pointed discussion I have agreed to keep working on this book but I want it on the record that it is under protest.

Finding the Right Driving Examiner

There will be a range of examiners working at your local test centre. But which of them is most likely to give your dog a driving licence?

Examiners with very poor eyesight

This could be your best bet. If you find an examiner who is able to see very little, they might not spot that they are being driven by a dog and will set off from the test centre quite happily with your pooch in the driver's seat. Even if they do eventually notice that it is a dog and not a hairy little person sitting next to them in the car, it will be too late. It will then be possible for you to bribe them into granting your dog a pass by threatening to reveal the weakness of their eyesight to their employers.

Examiners who are more generally vulnerable to bribery

Sometimes it is possible to bribe an examiner who has perfectly good eyesight but who has some other terrible secret. Amass suitable evidence against the examiner. For example, he/she may be an appalling alcoholic or drug addict. Perhaps they are secretly and shamefully unable to drive a car themselves. Or perhaps they just have an insatiable desire to repeatedly murder their driving candidates and dump their bodies in a quarry before returning to the centre alone claiming that the test had to be abandoned because of a particularly poor example of reverse parking. Threaten to reveal your evidence to the examiner's employers at the test centre and who knows, that elusive doggy driving licence could again be yours! On the other hand you could, of course, end up dumped in that quarry with the test candidates.[19] So practise some degree of caution if pursuing this option.

Examiners who are particularly gullible

If you're lucky you might just find a driving examiner who is so gullible that it will be possible to persuade him that, despite appearances, your dog is not in fact a dog but a diminutive, elderly, heavily bearded relative with particularly bad breath, a poor grasp of the English language and little in the way of thumbs.

---

19 Editor's note: Now there's an idea for what we could do with this author.

Examiners with significant neck injuries

If you are able to gain illegal access to medical records, you may find that one of your local driving examiners has experienced a significant trauma that has affected their neck. This is an occupational hazard for driving instructors who regularly suffer bumps, accidents or the effects of over-zealous emergency braking. Ideally what you need to find is an examiner whose neck has been injured in such a way that they are completely unable to turn their head to the right and see that there is a dog sitting in the driver's seat next to them rather than a human. Don't forget, if you are taking your test in a country where they drive on the other side of the road, you will need to find an examiner who cannot turn his head to the left.

Examiners who just really love dogs

Another very promising option to try. If you can find a driving examiner who really loves dogs, they may just take one look at your gorgeous pooch and give them a driving licence right there and then. It may not even be necessary for your dog to go through the rest of his driving test at all!

Examiners who really hate people

Conversely, examiners who have a hatred for other people may let your dog pass the driving test purely for the mayhem that will then be unleashed on the human race.[20]

---

20 *Editor's note: I know how they feel. Yes, let the mayhem be unleashed. It is the only way.*

Reasons for Wanting to Teach Your Dog How to Drive – No. 9

Your dog has already mastered riding a bike and operating your lawn mower

Blimey! You really have got an intelligent dog, haven't you? Be warned though, he may subsequently advance from cars to wanting to drive larger vehicles such as vans and lorries and will soon be pestering you to apply for his pilot's licence. And that could really cause panic among passengers during a flight.[21]

---

21 Editor's note: *Dear Sir/Madam, I would like to apply for the advertised position and enclose my CV.*

Reasons for Wanting to Teach Your Dog How to Drive – No. 10

You are extremely lazy

This is another poor excuse for teaching your dog to drive. Getting a dog through driver training takes real dedication and a great deal of time and effort. Those who are at all lazy are unlikely to be successful.

They will probably just throw their dogs into the front seat, switch on the ignition, sit back and hope for the best. And that's never going to work. Well, it might work but the car journey that follows will be quite short.

It is these sorts of people who give those of us who are serious about teaching our dogs to drive a bad name.[22]

_____

22 Editor's note: Dear Sir/Madam, I am really sorry about my last email, which contained a document about teaching dogs how to drive. I inadvertently attached a book that a colleague of mine is currently editing. This time, please find my CV attached.

Suitable Instruction Commands to Give Your Dog When He Is Driving

As with all dog training the commands and admonitions you give your dog during driving tuition must be fair, consistent and given at exactly the right moment. It's no good telling him 'Bad dog!' after he has caused a major pile-up.[23] You need to admonish him the moment he ploughs in to the side of another vehicle.

Nevertheless you should teach your dog to drive with kindness. Avoid admonishing him too severely for any traffic accidents that he causes. Remember your dog will wish to obey you. If your dog has caused a serious incident this will be your fault for one of the following reasons:

1. You failed to communicate your driving commands to your dog in a clear manner that he was able to understand;

---

23 Editor's note: Dear Mrs Davies, Yes, teaching dogs to drive is an incredibly irresponsible thing to do. I am trying to cancel the book, but the author turns out to have a really tight contract which is making life difficult for us all.

2. You failed to install dual controls in your car so you could stop the vehicle in the event of an emergency;

3. You put a dog in the driving seat of your car in the first place.

Whenever you are teaching your dog to do something, it is best to use short, clear, simple commands. 'Fetch,' 'sit,' 'heel,' 'roll over' and 'paw' are among the most popular verbal instructions used by dog owners.

Unfortunately, these commands are of limited use in the context of teaching a dog to drive. They may even be liable to misinterpretation.

Whatever you do, do not tell your dog to 'roll over' while he's at the controls of your car. He may respond by swinging the steering wheel round and mounting the kerb so the car somersaults across the road and lands upside down. And as his owner, you will be the one held responsible for this.

Nevertheless these sorts of commands give an idea of the type of simple monosyllabic instructions you should repeat increasingly loudly and firmly when your dog is driving. Commands such as 'drive,' 'left,' 'right' and 'stop' will be easily understood by your dog.

Phrases such as 'Could you take the fourth exit off the next roundabout,' 'turn sharp right at the next traffic lights and do a U-turn in front of Boots the Chemist' or 'watch out for that little old lady with the Zimmer frame crossing the road in front of you' will be less easily understood by your dog no matter how loudly you shout them.

Even worse, using commands such as these will probably confuse your dog and prove of little help to the old lady with the Zimmer frame.[24]

Instead you must find a way to communicate the essentials of driving to your dog using the simplest possible words. It may seem a challenge to get an animal to navigate through busy traffic by means of monosyllabic commands. If it helps, try to imagine your dog is a particularly unfriendly taxi driver or perhaps just a partner with whom you have spent an extremely long period of your life.

---

24 *Editor's note: Dear Mrs Davies, I am sorry to hear that, but I really didn't want your stupid job in the first place, so please stuff it where the sun don't shine.*

Once you have adopted this mental strategy, driving through traffic with only the occasional grunted single word of instruction will seem entirely natural.

Reasons for Wanting To Teach Your Dog
How To Drive – No. 11

You believe that your dog is insured to drive under the terms of the pet insurance you took out to cover his vet's fees

It is unusual for there to be a clause explicitly relating to car accidents within your pet insurance details. However, third-party insurance on your dog covers injuries and damage caused to others by your dog. This could (theoretically) cover car accidents caused by your dog running out into the road. So why shouldn't it cover car accidents caused by your dog while he is driving down the road?

Why not find out by becoming a test case? It might turn out that we could all get cheaper car insurance by taking out third-party liability pet insurance and leaving the driving to our dogs. It's got to be cheaper than fully comp motor insurance! Especially if you're under twenty-five years old (or 175 in dog years).

Also, maybe you are such a bad driver that insuring your dog to drive will cost less than insuring yourself.

For those of you who are extraordinarily bad

at driving and have a history of accidents and disqualifications to prove it, there must come a point where the insurance premiums available to you will be so phenomenally high it will be cheaper (if only marginally) to get motor insurance naming your dog as the main driver of your vehicle instead of yourself.

Teaching Very Small Dogs to Drive

Why should small dogs be denied the joy of driving?[25]

Regardless of size, dogs are a single species. If a Great Dane or Golden Retriever can jump in a car and drive it away why shouldn't a Chihuahua, a Pug, a miniature Scottish Terrier, a Papillion or a Cavalier King Charles Spaniel?

But there are some significant challenges facing the very small dog driver.

1. One slight problem is the fact that these dogs may be as little as eight inches high.

This means that when a Chihuahua is placed in the driving seat of an average sized car it is unable to see out the window and, even worse, it may have a pretty poor view of the steering wheel too.

2. If you try to solve this problem by picking your Chihuahua up and plonking him right onto the steering wheel then this will be the only one of the

---

25 Editor's note: I had dreams when I was little. I thought I'd be an astronaut or an ice-skater or something important and glamorous . . . How did it come to this?

car's controls that the animal will be capable of reaching. In fact, the average Chihuahua will have quite a bit of difficulty just stretching himself from one side of the steering wheel to the other.

3. Don't forget that steering a large, heavy vehicle may be challenging for a very small dog. If your dog has to stretch his entire body as far as it will go just to reach from one side of the steering wheel to the other, he is probably going to experience some difficulty turning the steering wheel to get the car round a tight corner.

4. Another problem is that turning the steering wheel sharply to get the car round a particularly tight corner will leave your tiny dog hanging completely upside down on the wheel. This may again restrict the dog's view of the road ahead.

5. It will also be difficult for your dog to turn a steering wheel if he is smaller than the steering wheel and is unable to make contact with anything else in the car other than the steering wheel.

6. If your dog only weighs 7 lb this will only add to the problems. Even though it is 3 ½ stone in dog weight.

7. The distance from the steering wheel to the gear level or brake pedal is the equivalent of a decent walk to a small dog.

Two immediately obvious solutions to these problems are:

1. Attaching stilts to your dog.

Simply attach artificial extensions to all of your tiny dog's limbs. This will leave your small dog with wooden or artificial poles several feet in length extending from each of his paws. He will thus resemble a very strange-looking greyhound or a particularly large spider.

One thing he will definitely be is ungainly. Driving a car is difficult enough for any dog. Driving a car for a small dog jammed onto the steering wheel while operating the rest of the controls using four pool cues strapped to his legs could represent a disaster waiting to happen.

Another point to remember is that a single pool cue weighs significantly more than a Chihuahua. Your miniature canine friend may therefore experience some difficulty trying to raise his leg extensions to change gear or to gently depress the pedals.[26]

2. Get a number of small dogs to work as a team.

A better option may be to bring together a pack of small dogs who can work together as a team to operate your car's controls. There is nothing unusual in this idea.

Huskies have been used for centuries to pull sleds together across the Arctic pack ice and using a pack of ten Chihuahuas to operate the controls of a Ford Focus is the obvious modern equivalent.

The specific positioning of the dogs on the controls should be arranged as you feel appropriate but a sensible arrangement would seem to be a single Chihuahua on each of the three pedals, another

---

26 Editor's note: How about making a robot costume for the dog, so he is like the tiny controller of a man-sized robot? Didn't think of that did you 'Dr Cesar Milligan'? (Though what imaginary educational establishment your 'doctorate' comes from I shudder to think.)

manning the handbrake, one to operate the indicators, headlights, windscreen wipers and back window de-mister button, one sitting on the dashboard to keep an eye on the road ahead, another on the back shelf to watch the road behind and the remaining three forming a canine pyramid on the driver's seat so they can reach and turn the steering wheel.[27]

Then, as long as your Chihuahuas are fully proficient at roadcraft, have been perfectly trained to work as a team and are capable of moving the handbrake using their 7 lb bodies, no problem should exist whatsoever.

---

27 *Editor's note: It worked in* Toy Story, *so why the hell not? In fact, why not make it a team of a hundred mice? Or a thousand cockroaches, all working together? That wouldn't be stupid at all, would it?*

Reasons for Wanting to Teach Your Dog How to Drive – No. 12

Your dog sits in front of the television wagging its tail whenever *Top Gear* is on

This is another of the less acceptable reasons for wanting to teach your dog to drive. There are, however, two reasons why your dog may enjoy watching *Top Gear*.

Firstly, his excitement will result from the fact that he has mistaken the presenters for three different breeds of dog. James May and Richard Hammond, with their lustrous hair, may appear to your dog as a large Afghan standing next to a little Lhasa Apso. Your dog may on the other hand see Jeremy Clarkson as a bulldog with the hairstyle of an ageing poodle.

The second reason that your canine companion may enjoy the show more than you is that, since he is a dog, he is blissfully unable to understand a single word these three overgrown mutts are saying.

What to Do If Your Dog Keeps Weeing Out of the Window

Always remember:

If your dog puts his front paw out of the window he is signalling for a turn.

If you dog puts his back paw out of the window he is about to do something else. Any vehicles passing you at the time are about to get a free screen wash. Why not try charging them a couple of quid for the privilege?[28]

---

28 Editor's note: One moment he's telling you the car window has to be up, the next down, the next it's back up again. MAKE YOUR MIND UP, YOU MORON! Ooo this sort of thing makes me so mad!

Essential Things to Have in the Car When Teaching Your Dog to Drive

Dual controls

These really are quite important.[29] If you're setting off on a journey with your dog in the driving seat you should certainly consider installing brake, accelerator and clutch pedals so you have access to them from the passenger seat.

A dual-control steering wheel on the passenger side might be a good idea as well.

---

29 Editor's note: So much so that they might have been worth mentioning right at the start of the book, but what do I know? I am a mere cog in a machine.

Some might argue that dual controls are not necessary and just decide to move all the controls from the driver's side in front of their dog over to the passenger side in front of themselves.

This, however, represents a loss of nerve on the part of the dog-driving trainer as well as a total waste of effort and money as a similar result can be achieved simply by swapping seats with your dog.

A plentiful supply of choccy drops

Many believe that the use of rewards such as food treats can provide significant help when teaching your dog basic obedience and simple commands. Tasty morsels may also therefore be useful while teaching your dog the intricacies of driving a car.

Each time your dog changes gear or negotiates a roundabout correctly, or avoids smashing into the back of a lorry, tell him 'Good boy!' and pop a doggy biscuit in his mouth. Pretty soon he will get the idea of how to drive through traffic.

Driving a car will, however, be one of the most difficult things your dog has ever had to master. Getting your dog just to understand how to read

road signs may require an extraordinary amount of doggy choc drops. You may therefore have to fill your vehicle with as many edible treats as you can fit in. Be warned, however: this technique may backfire.

If you pile the boot and back seat of your car high with dog treats, biscuits, bits of cheese and/or sausages, you will find it quite difficult to keep your dog's attention on the road in front of him.

Getting a dog to drive a car is a challenge at the best of times. Getting a dog to drive a car while he is constantly looking backwards over his shoulder at the mound of treats piled on the seat behind him will be significantly more difficult again.

Also, as mentioned earlier, the vast quantities of tasty treats will probably cause a correspondingly vast amount of drool to start flowing from your hound's mouth. This could create a significant hazard in the car. Slobber may, for example, fall across the pedals causing a danger of slippage when changing gear or braking. Alternatively, a gust from the window or air conditioning may cause a long stream of dribble to blow across your and/or your dog driver's faces making it difficult to see the road ahead.[30]

Training clicker

Rather than using treats to teach your dog how to drive, you may prefer to use a clicker-based method.

In the first instance, this involves priming your dog with a clicker. Give your dog a food treat every time he hears the sound of the click. Eventually, he will form a positive association with the clicking sound. When he hears the click, he will know he has done the right thing and that he will shortly be rewarded with a treat.

---

30 Editor's note: Do you ever feel like your life amounts to nothing? That the minutes and hours are stretching out ahead of you in an infinite spiral of pointlessness? How many summers have we left? AND I'M SPENDING THE LITTLE TIME I HAVE LEFT EDITING A FRIGGING BOOK ON TEACHING YOUR DOG TO DRIVE!?

Essential Things to Have In Your Car When Teaching Your Dog To Drive

Next, get in the car with your dog, get him to pull out into the traffic and click away every time he performs a correct driving manoeuvre. Obviously, you're going to need quite a loud clicker so your dog can hear the sound over the noise of the engine and the roar of the rest of the traffic around you.

Also, if your dog drives you into a wall or another car, the impact may cause you to accidentally press on the clicker. Your dog will then hear the click and make the obvious deduction that driving into the wall or the other car was precisely the thing that you wanted him to do. And if your dog starts thinking like that, it could prove disastrous for his driving career.

Another problem with using the clicker method is that a number of functions on your car may make a similar clicking noise. The sound of the indicator clicking away may cause your dog to think he has done something very good indeed. He will then become incredibly excited and assume that you are about to give him the entire vast quantity of treats that are piled up behind you on the back seat.[31]

---

31 *Editor's note: So what is the point of . . . Oh, I can't be bothered any more.*

MOT, driving licence, insurance details

In case you get stopped by the police when your dog is driving you should ensure you have all necessary documentation to hand. These will include your car's MOT, your dog's driving licence and his insurance certificate.

Your dog's vaccination certificates from the vet, as well as any awards he has received for obedience or agility training, may also be useful.

Just thrust a bundle of suitable-looking literature through the window at the policeman and hope for the best.

On the other hand it's quite unlikely your dog will stop the car no matter how hard any law enforcement officer starts waving at you.

So all being well the situation simply will not arise.

Disguise kit and dressing-up clothes

However, let's assume you do get stopped by the police. At this point they may take a close look at your dog's insurance and licence documents.

As we have already seen it is quite difficult to obtain a full driving licence and motor insurance for your dog.[32] You may therefore have had to be slightly economical with the truth when applying for these items.

One area in which you may have stretched the truth in your licence application is regarding your dog's species. In a moment of confusion you may have told the DVLA and your insurance company that he was human rather than canine.

But do not worry! When flagged down by the police quickly reach into your in-car make up and disguise kit and pop a hat, wig, sunglasses, etc. on your canine driver. In this way your dog should better resemble the human person depicted on their forged driving licence photo card.

And thus any problems with the police should be quickly averted!

---

32 *Editor's note: I'm finding it hard to breathe. Is it hot in here?*

Is It a Problem If Your Dog Can Only See in Black and White?

The fact that dogs can only see in black and white presents a problem for them when driving. Particularly when they have to stop at traffic lights.

To your dog the traffic light colours will appear as grey, grey and grey. How is your poor mutt supposed to know when he should stop and when he should go?

On the plus side, whenever he is driving he will probably just drive straight through the junction and ignore the lights completely in any case.

For similar reasons he will also probably ignore the blue flashing lights coming up behind you.

Why Does My Dog Look Worried When I Ask Him to Put the Car Into Neutral?

This may be because your dog has misheard you and thought you said something about being neutered.

You will be able to confirm this is what happened if he does an abrupt U-turn and starts driving at maximum speed in the opposite direction from the vet's.

How to Get Your Dog Through the Written Section of the Driving Test?

As we may have mentioned, acquainting your dog with the Highway Code and the written examination may be tricky.[33]

Let's not beat around the bush, no matter how intelligent your dog, no matter how patient you are, no matter how many choccy drops you use to encourage him, you're going to have your work cut out getting your dog through the written driving test. There are three reasons for this.

1. Dogs cannot read.

2. Dogs cannot write.

3. Even if you can teach your dog to read or write, they lack opposable thumbs. They therefore have great difficulty gripping a biro to fill in their answers on the written driving test.

---

33 Editor's note: I mean I really can't breathe, and my heart is beating really fast . . . And it feels like the walls are closing in on me.

By all means have a go at teaching your dog to read
and write but bear in mind that the current rate of
achievement for this is 100% failure (that's 700% in
terms of dog failure).

And that's not just for those of us trying to teach dogs to drive today. That's for all humans ever during the entirety of history. No one has ever managed to teach a dog to read and write since the first domestication of the wolf. I am working on a system to address this problem, but there is a lot to be done.[34]

Happily, in recent times the powers-that-be have at last paid heed to the concerns of the dog-driving community. The written driving test can now be done online, which makes it much easier for dog candidates to key in their answers.

---

34 Editor's note: And where did all those little dogs come from? Tiny dogs everywhere, swarming all over the place? Look! There's a little pink one!

How to Disguise Yourself as a Dog and Take the Written Test for Him

If you are having limited success teaching your dog to read and write but wish to get him through the written driving test, another option may exist.

A more effective means of getting your dog through the written test may be to disguise yourself as a dog and sit the exam yourself.[35]

Disguising yourself as your dog is a useful skill to develop as it may come in handy on other occasions in your animal's driving career. These may include your dog's appearances in court for driving offences he has committed or at driver-training classes issued for driving offences against him in lieu of penalty points on his licence.

In such eventualities it may be better for you to attend rather than your dog. And when you attend it may be better for you to wear a disguise so you resemble your dog. If you wear some sort of onesie, remember to choose one that resembles your dog and then you can quickly slip in and out of your disguise.

---

35 Editor's note: Little pink dogs . . . biting my ankles . . . chewing my toes . . .

Or for those on a budget, collect all that unwanted hair your dog leaves lying around your house and that fills your vacuum cleaner every day, spread it out on the floor in front of you, strip yourself completely naked, coat yourself in some form of adhesive and roll around in the hair until all parts of your body are covered with the dog hair.

You can then choose how to proceed from the following two options. Either you can use your disguise to actually pretend to be your dog. Or you can use your dog-like disguise to persuade people that you are a human who just happens to be covered in dog-like fur and who is therefore regularly mistaken for a dog. Particularly when you are driving.

If you opt to pretend you really are a dog, you should behave in a suitably doggy manner. Walk around on all fours, show a strong interest in sniffing anything you come across, regularly cock your leg for a quick wee, occasionally wolf down some absolutely disgusting-looking item that you have found discarded on the floor and don't forget to turn round in a circle three times prior to sitting down.

How to Disguise Yourself as a Dog and Take the Written Test for Him

Do bear in mind, however, that if you attend a court hearing in the guise of your dog and you are found guilty, the punishment you are handed down may be unexpectedly severe.

The death penalty no longer exists in this country for humans, but it does in certain circumstances remain in force for dogs. If you (in the guise of your dog) are found guilty of even a minor driving offence, the court may decree that you are taken from the court to a veterinary practice where you will pay the ultimate price for your misdeeds. Or even worse you may find yourself sentenced to being castrated.

It is therefore probably advisable to use your disguise to pretend you are a dog-like human who is covered in hair. The worst that can happen then is that you are given a fine for your bad driving.

Although you may also receive a suspended sentence for appearing completely naked in a court of law save for an inadequate covering of glue and discarded dog hair.[36]

---

36 Editor's note: Please stop the little dogs. I can feel them crawling up my spine and into my ears . . . they're inside my head . . . they're taking me over, I tell you . . .

Disguising Yourself as a Dog – Some Do's and Don'ts

In case you prefer to take the risk on pretending to be an actual dog, here are a few hints on how best to approach the task:

- <u>Do</u> try to act in a friendly dog-like manner.
- <u>Don't</u> immediately go for the jugular of anyone with whom you get into a minor argument.

- <u>Do</u> allow other dogs to sniff your bottom.
- <u>Don't</u> get so used to sniffing other people's bottoms you carry on doing it even when you're no longer wearing your dog disguise.

- <u>Do</u> communicate using dog-like woofs, growls and whimpers.
- <u>Don't</u> give the game away by trying to speak in normal English but with a dog-like accent so you end up sounding like Scooby-Doo.[37]

---

37 *Editor's note: Actually, I'm feeling a bit better now. Maybe it was just an anxiety attack.*

- <u>Do</u> learn to act in an appropriately sociable manner when meeting other dogs.
- <u>Don't</u> immediately mount other dogs and start humping away. Again, particularly remember to avoid this if you're not wearing your dog disguise at the time. Also do not hump people's legs because you think it will make you look more dog-like as the vibration caused by the humping may cause your disguise to slip off and give the game away.

- <u>Do</u> spend a lot of your time sniffing things you find.
- <u>Don't</u> look up from a good sniff to comment, 'Pooo-eeee! This is completely minging!'

- <u>Do</u> practise grooming yourself in a suitably dog-like manner.
- <u>Don't</u> put your back out and get stuck while attempting to lick your own genitals.

- **<u>Do</u>** hold up one of your doggy paws when someone says, 'Paw!' to you.[38]
- **<u>Don't</u>** say 'Pleased to meet you I'm sure' as you do so.

- **<u>Do</u>** pant constantly.
- **<u>Don't</u>** do this when you phone people as it may give them the wrong impression.

38 Editor's note: In fact I'm feeling splendid, positively serene.

Reasons for Wanting to Teach Your Dog How to Drive – No. 13

You know you only passed your own driving test through sheer luck and in your heart of hearts you know you are a terrible driver

This really is not a very good reason at all. Indeed, it may not go down at all well if you offer it as an excuse to a police officer who has pulled you over after spotting a dog is sitting in the driving seat of your car.[39]

---

39 Editor's note: *I'm not sure I've ever felt better. It's like everything around me is weightless and floating away into space.*

Reasons for Wanting to Teach Your Dog How to Drive – No. 14

It will help you pick up members of the opposite sex

Being driven around by your dog will certainly attract the attentions of the opposite sex, although they may be unwilling to actually get in the car with you. It will, however, look extremely cool if you draw up alongside them sitting in the back of a top of the range BMW driven by a beautifully groomed, perfectly controlled, pedigree dog in a chauffeur's cap.

Bear in mind that it will look less cool if you arrive screaming and thrashing around in terror trying to control an excitable hairy mongrel at the wheel of a thirty-year-old Reliant Robin that has just driven through the side of their garden shed. (And that's a 210-year-old Reliant Robin in dog years).

Reasons for Wanting to Teach Your Dog How to Drive – No. 15

You have bet an acquaintance a large amount of money that your dog can drive

This is another of the dodgier excuses for dog-driver training. The amount of money wagered will have to be very significant to cover the costs of teaching your dog to drive, buying a new car every few journeys, bribing local policemen and driving instructors, etc.

On the other hand if you have a friend with significantly more money than sense, it's another reason to get Fido into the driver's seat!

So You've Successfully Got Your Dog a Driving Licence – Now What?

Your dog is back from the test centre. He's successfully got through the test. He's got his licence clamped in his mouth. His tail is wagging like mad behind him. He's just cocked his leg up over your car to inform you that he now owns it.[40]

As a special treat, why not take this opportunity to let him have his discarded old 'L' plates so he can spend a few minutes chewing them up and tearing them into tiny little pieces?

But now your dog is officially qualified to drive, where is he going to go, what's he going to do with the car and what care should you take as the responsible owner of a driving dog?

---

40 *Editor's note: Dear colleagues, I'm sorry I have been acting strangely lately, but I'm feeling a lot better now. I will however be leaving soon. I am going to move to Tahiti to take up an exciting opportunity that came to me in a dream recently. I will be building a fleet of tiny robot Chihuahuas who will form the basis of a new world economy, of which I will be supreme leader . . .*

Agility Courses for Your Driving Dog

Dogs love to go to agility training lessons, where they can enjoy racing round in a field, going through tunnels, weaving in and out of poles, leaping over small jumps and running up and down see-saws.

It is natural therefore that your dog will want to perform similar agility exercises while driving a car. Suitable locations in which to practise agility exercises in a car can easily be found on public highways or in the areas immediately surrounding public highways.

If your dog enjoys weaving in and out of a set of poles, think of the pleasure he will get from driving your Vauxhall Frontera in and out of a set of street lights. Just find a long enough stretch of road with street lights along its edge. Please note the distances between the street lights should be sufficient to drive a medium to large vehicle between them and there shouldn't be too many pedestrians on the pavement at the time. Or at least there should be sufficient room for the pedestrians to leap out of the way as your dog begins his driving slalom in and out of the lamp posts.

Tunnels for your dogs to drive down are found on many roads or, if you have a small enough car and you find the exposed end of a pipe, your dog might enjoy going on a short tour of the local water pipes and sewage system.

And for the thrill of going over a see-saw or leaping over a series of small jumps, why not try getting your dog to drive the car and leap it over a bascule bridge, such as Tower Bridge in London, just as it is raising? [41]

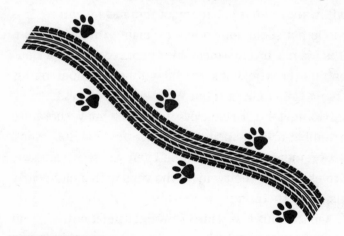

41 *Senior editor's note: The previous editor of this book is no longer employed by this company. He has been removed from his post following an ugly incident with a toy car smeared with meat paste and is now under medical supervision.*

Chasing Things In the Car

Many people ask me what they should do when their dog keeps chasing things when they're out driving in the car. My answer is, 'Get used to it!'

Dogs like chasing things. It could be a ball, a cat or just an injured pensioner trying to make it to safety. If it moves, your dog will chase it.

When your dog is out driving on the road, he will be surrounded by hundreds of moving objects and will want to chase as many of them as he can.

Do not scold your dog for chasing things in a car. It is his natural instinct. But of course now that he is behind the wheel of a car, he will have a much better chance of catching them.[42]

Going for a drive with your dog may therefore resemble a high-speed car chase from a Hollywood action movie. Things will be even worse if someone drives past on their way to the vet's with a cat clearly visible in their car.

On the plus side, think how exciting it will be to go screeching around in your car with your dog at the wheel performing high-speed stunts and turns.

---

42 *Senior editor's note: Dear, oh dear, what has been going on here?*

Getting Your Driving Dog to Come Back to You

Now that your dog is driving he will enjoy using the car to chase after many more things than was previously possible. But don't forget, your dog will now be able to chase them at much higher speeds and for much longer distances than if he were travelling on paw.

You may therefore find yourself being contacted by road patrol officers asking you to come and collect your dog, whom they have found sitting in a car having run out of petrol several hundred miles from your home.

As a result you may have to make occasional trips to remote parts of the country to get your dog (and his car) back.[43]

In order to avoid this you should ideally train your dog to return to you. Recall is, however, difficult with a driving dog. The normal practice employed by dog owners is to call, 'Here, boy!' or to use some

---

43 *Senior editor's note: Just to note that we have serious concerns about the entire content of this book. We are urgently looking into options for delaying or cancelling publication.*

sort of whistle to get their animals to return to them. You can try this but it may be ineffective if your dog is driving away from you in a car. You will have to shout or blow your whistle incredibly hard to make yourself heard over the roar of your dog's 2.5 litre (17.5 in dog litres) engine as he disappears up the motorway at 100 mph (700 mph in dog mph).

Other owners use a training lead to teach their dogs to come back to them. Again, this works well when both the owner and their dog are on foot. But it works much less well when one or other of them is in a fast-moving vehicle. If your dog is accelerating to anything more than 4 mph (28 dmph) in the car, then trying to yank him back with a long lead will be an uncomfortable experience for both you and your dog.

It is only safe to keep your driving dog on a lead if you are sitting alongside him in the car's passenger seat. Then you can give the occasional gentle tug on the lead to bring him under control, to get him to return home or to stop him from driving through next door's garden.

Recall may also be achieved by installing some form of walkie-talkie system in your car. You can then shout, 'Here boy!' to him even when he is several miles from home. Be careful, though, if you use a mobile phone for the same purpose. If you do you will have to ensure that your dog can operate it 'paws free' while he is driving.

One thing you should certainly avoid is teaching your dog to put fuel into the car himself. If your dog knows how to re-fuel the vehicle and sets off in hot pursuit of another car carrying a cat, you may never see him again.

Even more important: never let your dog have your bank payment card or tell him your PIN.

A Final Note on Safety for Your Dog In the Car

Finally, and most importantly: do not ever allow your dog to drive with the windows wound up. Particularly not if he is driving on a hot day. Remember – dogs can die in hot cars. And this is will be even worse if your dog happens to be driving the car at the time he dies. Don't forget that your dog will have little or no understanding of how the car's air conditioner works. Not only that but the car's air conditioner will probably be clogged up as a result of having treats and bits of meat smeared all over it during the early stages of your dog's driving tuition. Carefully observing safety rules such as these is key to a long, active, safe and happy driving career for your dog and his screaming passengers.[44]

Oh, and another very good reason for having the windows open while your dog is driving is because you may suddenly need to use them as an emergency exit.

---

44 *Senior editor's note: If for any reason this book ever does see the light of day, please remember that all the advice in it is awful, it has been edited by a deluded, pathetic individual and in any reasonable world we would have been allowed to cancel it. Also, if you happen to come across any miniature robot Chihuahuas, please contact your local law enforcement agency as soon as possible.*

But don't have the windows open too much or your dog will stick his head out. [45]

---

45 *Senior editor's note: Hang on! One minute the author tells you the windows are meant to be up, the next down, the next up again. Ooo, this kind of inconsistency makes me so mad!*

Notes on Dog's Driving Progress

_____

_____

_____

_____

_____

_____

_____

_____

_____

_____

Notes on Accidents and Associated Insurance Claims

_____

_____

_____

_____

_____

_____

_____

_____

_____

_____

More Notes on Accidents and Associated Insurance Claims

Details of injuries sustained on other drivers by dog attacks following accidents, threats issued, associated insurance claims and action taken by Police and RSPCA

_____

_____

_____

_____

_____

_____

_____

_____

Acknowledgements

Thanks to Hugh Barker, Clive Hebard and Dominic Wakeford at Constable and Robinson and Simon Buchanan at Design 23.

Thanks also to Richard Hocknell for the photos
to Eleanor Haskins for lots of the other photos
and to Andy Jacobson for general pictorial assistance, the dog driving licence and the 'Shofur' hat

And thanks for additional pictures to:
John Tierney and Jemma Tierney
John Hazler
Deb Hampson (and Henry the British Bulldog)
Bob and Elaine Spencer and Adam and Gill Bullen (and Henry the Lakeland Terrier)
Chris Naylor (and Bruce the black Labrador)
Isobel Roberts (and Izzy the Lhasa Apso)
Neptune Car Spares Ltd, Birkenhead

Thanks to principal canine models Dylan and Lily (assisted by Bertie)
And thanks to human models Clive Hinton, Eleanor Haskins and "Blind" Andy Jacobson